THE
4 KEYS
TO INFLUENCE

Learn the 4 basic principles that make the most powerful

people in the world so influential and create a path to

reach your personal vision for success

CONTENTS

From Lamb to Bam! My Story.

Catchy title right? I got that little tidbit from a woman who visited one of my networking events. I told my story of transforming from an extreme wallflower to a networking queen and it really resonated with her. She said she wanted me to help her have a transformation like I did. She told me to transform her from Lamb to Bam! Clearly the concept stuck with me.

My story begins at birth as all others do. I was the little girl who stayed in her room playing with toys alone, rarely begged for a play date and could often be found riding my bicycle alone up and down the street making up stories inside my head.

I'm the quiet girl, the introvert, the loner. I've always had just a few close friends and was fine with a small circle of people whom I'd call on only when I wanted an outing such as bowling or to see a movie.

I wasn't a total loner. I did join clubs, was a member of the marching band, and helped build floats in school. But when it came to making close friends, going to parties, and knowing where to sit in the cafeteria — that's where I struggled.

For the first 20 years of my life I let my introversion rule me. I rarely went to parties and when I did, I stuck by the person who brought me and rarely ventured off to talk with others. I was uncomfortable in groups and had no idea how to introduce myself, let alone carry small talk. I convinced myself that I just didn't like people and accepted that networking would never be "for me."

As I became an adult and entered the job market, I started to realize how much value was placed on extroverted skills. Sales associates who engage with customers rather than cling to the cash registers are rewarded with more hours and opportunities for management, employees who network and build relationships with managers were given privilege of first choice in the projects they took on.

Me, I kept getting passed over for opportunities because others were more popular and more gregarious than I. I knew I was quick witted, educated, and competent, but none of that matters when you haven't formed a connection with the people who make decisions on your behalf.

Meanwhile, I found myself in love with the most extroverted and charismatic man I've ever met. He made friends wherever he went, people admired him, and he had the ability to quickly build rapport with strangers. Together we were an incomparable match, but for each of us, the differences created frustration when it came to social experiences.

MY TRANSFORMATION

The catalyst for my transformation was our 2nd day of pre-marital counseling. We had taken a personality test and our pastor reviewed the results with us. I tested highly introverted, while my husband tested highly extroverted. Once the results were revealed my husband gave a huge "aha" and admitted that he never understood why my personality seemed to leave the building when I walked into a crowded room. He described how he would tell people how amazing I was, but then they'd meet me in person and feel let down because I didn't meet expectations. This new understanding was met with tears and the realization that it was finally time to make a change. I needed to find a way to show the world my personality even though I lost my energy when engaging with others.

STRATEGY

Any type of transformation needs a strategy, Mine was three fold:

1) I asked my husband to teach me everything he knew about networking. I wanted to learn to shake a hand, make small talk, and keep the attention of a crowd. He proved to be an amazing mentor and taught me all that he knew that could help me on my path.

2) I took advantage of my job in experiential marketing and used it as an opportunity to practice all of my new techniques. When I went for an event, I practiced connecting with people, being the life of the party, and even

dancing. I often did promotional events with "Captain Morgan," an actor who wore a costume during events to market a rum product. We were both very introverted and shy, so we agreed to help support each other on our journey to learn to become better connectors.

3) I read books on charisma, influence, and even the art of war. I also studied body language and the psychology of social groups.
And finally, I practiced my craft for many years, being cognizant at all times of the perceptions others may have of me during social gatherings and asking for feedback from others as much as possible.

THE RESULT

Today, I'm a pro at working a room, I can connect with almost anyone, and I have an engaged network. I accomplished this by practicing the behaviors that lead to influence, while making sure to stay within my personal comfort zone and giving myself plenty of "introversion time" between social engagements.

My mission is to find others who are like me and show them that they don't have to settle for being passed over just because they're introverted, shy, or simply don't know how to connect with others at a high level. Most of all, I want everyone to know how to showcase their value, so others see the amazing gifts they have to offer.

Creating Your Vision

Powerful, impactful, and influential; these are the descriptors you want to define you.

Getting there is a journey, but it's absolutely within your reach to become the powerful individual you were meant to be. By understanding the basic rules of human connection and making small changes everyday, you can learn to influence others in ways you never imagined.

To begin your journey, it's important to first determine what you desire in life. Take the time to reflect and imagine yourself in the future.

What does your future self look like? What has that person accomplished? Picture the positive comments you receive from others. What do they say about you?

Use that image to create your vision. What's your vision of a more influential you?

The key to this exercise is true honesty. Take the time to really dig deep into what you want for yourself. This is not the time to compile a list of things you "should" be doing based on a preconception you have. This is the time to consider what you really want from your life.

What does your future self look like?

_____

_____

What do people say about you?

_____

_____

What have you accomplished?

_____

_____

How do you spend your time?

_____

_____

What do you look forward to?

_____

_____

What are you proud of?

_____

_____

Now it's time to evaluate where you are in relation to your goal. Take the time to truly consider your current state and create a baseline for your transformation.

Be as descriptive as possible so you can easily picture yourself today when you review this workbook years into the future.

How do you see yourself today in comparison to your ultimate goal?

_____

_____

_____

On a scale of 1-10 with 10 being your ultimate vision for yourself, what number are you at now? _____

How do you feel about yourself today?

_____

_____

_____

What are you currently struggling with?

_____

_____

_____

What does your career look like?

_____

_____

_____

What does your social life look like?

_____

_____

_____

What are you doing that gets in the way of reaching your goals?

_____

_____

_____

What are you doing that gets you closer to your goals?

_____

_____

_____

What are you most proud of today?

_____

_____

_____

What is Influence?

The word "influence" can be a loaded concept for many of us. When I ask others what an influential person looks like they often list people such as Gandhi, Martin Luther King, and Marilyn Monroe. Our vision of influence is typically very high level and largely out of reach for most people.

One of the most important values I would like to impart onto you is that influential people are everywhere, not just in the highest ranks of society. Influential people choose their story and create a life that works for them. They are in control of their surroundings and their own destiny and they choose deliberately where they will go next.

In this book, the definition of influence is:

> Exhibiting personal control over your environment through the use of persuasive techniques, personal goal-setting and visualization.

I will teach you effective ways to influence your environment and get what you want from life by persuading others to give you what you need. These techniques do not cause people to act outside of their own will, but rather inspires them to help you willingly and enthusiastically.

Presence

One of my favorite sayings is "those who look the part get the opportunity to audition for the role." I'm not sure where that saying originates from, but the truth within the saying is extremely powerful.

Rarely do we see people appointed to a position of power that don't look like the role they are taking on, so it's important that you prioritize fitting your external presence to the goals you've set out to achieve.

For example, if you're interested in becoming a personal trainer, others must first be able to envision you filling that role. What a personal trainer looks like in their minds will play a major part in determining whether or not they will choose you.

The reason for this is simply trust. We trust experiences that fit into our perceptions of reality and we reward those who confirm our expectations.

This is not to say you cannot create your own style and expression, but you'll find the fastest route to success is to develop your style within the framework already set.

Therefore as a personal trainer for example, you should look fit, wear fitness clothing, and talk about health and wellness; but to express yourself you may choose to dye your hair orange, or wear goggles. You've still fit within the framework of a personal trainer, but you've also given yourself the freedom of creative expression to make it your own.

Similarly if you happen to be in the roofing industry you'll likely wear construction boots, a tool belt, and overalls or denim jeans; but you may choose to carry pink tools or wear red construction boots rather than traditional tan. You may also have a unique way of serving your customers that makes you stand out amongst others in your industry.

In addition to the way we look at first glance, our presence also involves the way we behave. No matter what your goals are, having a powerful presence will make you more influential and increase the likelihood that others will give you what you want.

One of the major keys to a powerful presence is mastering your own non-verbal communication. As humans, the majority of the messages we receive when communicating with one another are non-verbal. This means that we're always taking in messages — from the context of the conversation, to the tone of voice of the speaker, to the physical gestures being used to convey a message.

The words being used are actually the least important piece of information being taken in during a conversation.

So how can you maximize your non-verbal communication to be more influential?

Improving your non-verbal communication starts with the awareness that others are making assumptions about us at all times based on what they see, hear and feel. This is not to be taken personally, but you should always be aware of what others may be thinking when

> "AS HUMANS, THE MAJORITY OF THE MESSAGES WE RECEIVE WHEN COMMUNICATING WITH ONE ANOTHER ARE NON-VERBAL."

you're communicating with them. Here's a few things to consider:

Body Language: Being an influential communicator means showing others that you're interested in them and have the power to make an impact in their life. This means using powerful body language and connecting with them at a deeply human level. Here's what you should pay attention to:

> Eye Contact - Try to look your partner in the eyes about 70% of the time you're speaking with them. To do this, look for the color of their eyes about every 10 seconds or so, then you can look away or draw down slightly to their nose. Make sure to keep a relaxed eye-gaze. Too much eye contact can be intimidating.

Eye contact has several purposes. First, we know that those who are untrustworthy (liars) often find it difficult to look us in the eyes, so we look at eye contact as a signifier of trustworthiness.

Eye contact also gives us power. People at a lower level often spend more time looking away or casting their eyes to the floor. This is programmed in us as a sign of respect and reverence to those in power. If you want to be seen as powerful, you'll need to give straight-forward, confident eye contact when engaging with others.

Lastly, eye contact connects us. True intimacy starts with eye contact and feeling comfortable with that level of intimacy will allow you to establish valuable bonds with others. People are generally more likely to help those they care about. Your eye contact can help you build incredible bonds that allow you to benefit from the relationship quickly.

Handshakes - Look your conversation partner in the eyes, posture your shoulders back slightly, reach out your right hand for theirs, connect the webs of your hands (between the thumb and forefinger) and pump 3 times before releasing.

The significance of a handshake is the connecting power of physical touch. The origins of the handshake began with trust-building. It is said that the first handshakes were more like a pat down, where rival leaders would check to ensure no weapons were hidden in the hands of their enemy. Once they were sure they were safe, they could continue the exchange.

Today, a handshake is still a representation of trust. It establishes you as an ally willing to show your hand. And just like eye contact, the more we touch, the more we connect emotionally with others.

Stance - When you want to build an alliance with another person it's important to show them your dedication to the relationship. By focusing your energy on them for an extended period of time you build trust, show them they are valuable to you, and keep them engaged in the conversation.

When interacting with people, make sure your body is always facing towards them. Your body points in the direction it wants to be, so if your body parts are aimed for the door, your communication partner subconsciously knows you don't want to talk with them. When you're ready to leave a conversation, gently touch the back of a hand, shoulder, or arm and politely let the person know you're ready to move on.

It's also important to be aware that the way you stand sends signals about how powerful you are. Powerful people stand up straight and take up more space with their body, so avoid folding into yourself.

To take up more space, try opening your feet up to shoulder width apart. That's a great stance for taking up additional space without getting carried away. You can also do things such as stretching your arms across a nearby empty seat, which makes you appear larger.

Smiling - Smiling is so powerful that it makes us happier, even if we didn't feel happy before we started smiling. To be an expert smiler, practice authentic smiles at home by making mental notes or setting reminders to smile for 10 seconds each day. Think about the last time you were truly happy and engaged and allow yourself to feel the authentic joy of the moment. By practicing this, you'll teach yourself how to smile on command.

You can also make smiling a habit when talking on the phone even though others can't see you. A smile is so powerful, we can sense it through our digital mediums.

Why is this important? Smiling (with purpose) can be a powerful tool to build relationships and establish powerful alliances. The goal is not to smile all of the time, but to use your smile as a tool to connect with special people.

Smiling at another person makes them feel important, valuable and impactful. When you smile at them, they believe you enjoy their presence and appreciate what they have to offer.

<u>Lighting up for others</u> - "Lighting up" describes the elevation of energy that you feel when you see someone you truly care about and are excited to see. People care about those who care about them, so by lighting up for others they will be more likely to feel a stronger connection to you.

Lighting up takes practice and is a high-level body language skill. To make this a part of your regular interactions, you'll need to practice getting in the mindset of gratitude and being thankful for the people you interact with. When you truly feel grateful for them, it will show up in your body language in all the right ways.

Body Language Activities

Activity 1 Eye Contact - Learning to look people in the eyes for long periods of time can be uncomfortable at first. It takes hours of practice to succeed. For this exercise, you'll find a friend that you trust and request that they complete an exercise with you.

Place chairs across from each other and when you are ready to begin set the timer on your smartphone, watch or computer. Look each other in the eyes for 60 seconds without interruption. Practice this until you feel so comfortable doing it that there are rarely giggles or squirms of discomfort.

Activity 2 Lighting Up - Lighting up and showing vibrance and vitality when entering a room requires genuine emotion. Our body language sensors are highly evolved and can detect even the slightest bit of inauthenticity. To make sure you show up with authentic vibrance, you'll need to practice gratitude and visualize yourself feeling a connection to each person you plan to connect with and receiving great value from the interaction.

The next time you plan to visit a networking event, gathering, or friendly meeting with a new person, take a few minutes before the interaction to picture the incredible value you are about to receive just by meeting them.

<u>Activity 3 Stance</u> - Powerful people take up space and are steady in their movements. To get comfortable with this, practice standing with an uncomfortably wide stance and claiming a large space for yourself. Do this while holding incredibly still and imagining yourself in a room full of people moving quickly as you stand completely still in the midst of the chaos. This will help you to comfortably settle into a power stance when in public.

Another great way to increase your power is to take on a power pose. A power pose involves making a V with your arms and an upside down V with your legs. Spread them greater than shoulder length apart to get the full effect. You may also choose to stand like Superman, which is also a form of power posing.

<u>Activity 4 Smiling</u> - Smiling can be an excellent way to build greater connection with others and gain favor with those you seek to engage with, but in order to achieve these benefits the smile must appear authentic. An inauthentic smile can create distrust and cause the person you are engaging with to believe you have ill intentions or simply do not like them.

To practice smiling use a smartphone camera to capture your practice. To get started, visualize the last time you were extremely happy and engaged. Remember the way you felt in that moment. In front of the camera, try to create an authentic smile. Compare your attempt with a real photo from that moment, or ask a friend for feedback.

Presence Planner

Now it is time to put your new tips into action. What can you do today to improve your personal presence?

_____

_____

_____

_____

_____

How can you improve your body language?

_____

_____

_____

_____

Are you dressing like the job you want? What can you do to look the part?

_____

_____

_____

_____

Authority

If you've ever seen an episode of Game of Thrones or watched an old western movie, you'll know that the most respected kings and the legendary cowboys built their reputations over time. Similarly, today's leaders must build their reputation through a strong track record of success and knowledge in their sphere of influence.

People follow those who can prove their expertise and they are even more likely to follow if you receive an endorsement from a high-level peer that has already built a successful network.

Take the time to do a little research to find out what the most powerful people in your industry did to achieve their level of influence and create a plan for how you too can attain the level of power you want to achieve.

> "YOU NEED A TRACK RECORD OF SUCCESS IN YOUR INDUSTRY AND RECOMMENDATIONS FROM QUALITY SOURCES WHO HAVE THE POWER TO SUPPORT YOUR GROWTH."

For example, if your goal is to become an executive at the company you work for you'll want to interview some executives you admire to ask them how they reached success. Then you'll take that advice and use it to craft your plan for how you will reach your personal goals for success. Every path is unique, so don't be alarmed if your story is already quite different from the people you talk with. The important thing is to find out the key catalysts for their growth and learn about their failures, so you can try to avoid the same missteps.

Building your authority is a lot like building your resume. You need a track record of success in your industry and recommendations from quality sources. You can also think of this as your personal brand.

If you're new to an industry, you may need to build your resume by offering services for free to influential people. Always be strategic with your time and energy when building your reputation. You don't want to burn yourself out in the building phase and lack the energy you need when you've arrived at your destination.

Set requirements for the people you help for free. Make sure that each person you engage with fits the criteria you have set and ask them for a trade if they're happy with the work you've done.

For example, as a marketer you may offer to create a free digital campaign for someone whose business has 10,000 Twitter followers. Your trade would involve you completing the campaign for them and in return they share 10 tweets during a one month period promoting your business and write a recommendation for your LinkedIn profile.

List 3 people who are highly influential in your industry. How did they become so powerful?

Person 1

_____

_____

Person 2

_____

_____

Person 3

_____

_____

Are there similarities between you and any of those influential people? What lessons can you gain from them?

_____

_____

_____

_____

_____

_____

Is there anyone who can validate or legitimize your authority? How can you get to know them? What value can you offer that person to build a sustainable relationship?

_____

_____

_____

_____

Who could become your mentor? How can you engage them as a mentor? What can you offer them in return?

_____

_____

_____

_____

What are 3 things you can do within the next 6 months to build your credibility?

1_____

2_____

3_____

Visibility & Consistency

People always tend to favor the familiar. The reason for this is very simple. As humans, we are more likely to trust things we've had a great deal of exposure to because we know they are safe. In our historic past, it was important to know our surroundings and to be wary of new people or places. If we weren't, the consequences could be fatal. By sticking with the familiar we can trust that we probably won't die from our encounter.

Can you imagine walking into the villages of the past and saying hello? Would you expect to be greeted with open arms or would the villagers likely raise their spears demanding an explanation for your visit?

> "As humans, we are more likely to trust things we've had exposure to, because we know they are safe."

In modern society, we may not carry spears, but we are still naturally distrustful of people we've just met. This is why it is necessary to develop a plan for how you will become so consistently visible to your audience that it's easy for them to trust you.

Without trust you're more likely to encounter barriers when you're engaging with people. You'll need their trust if you want to persuade them to help you, buy from you, or hire you.

Here's a simple example of consistency and visibility in the corporate world:

Cassie is a Call Center Manager who wants to be considered for the next Operations Director position. In order to be considered, she'll need to catch the eyes of two VP's of Operations who rarely interact with people on her level.

Cassie learned that there are three committees that help brainstorm ideas for making the Call Center more efficient. She also learned that the VP's attend committee meetings regularly and also review the minutes from meetings they missed.

To build her visibility, Cassie decided to join the committee that best fit her schedule and was most relevant for showing off her understanding of overall operations strategy. Once she joined, she blocked off her calendar to ensure that she could make the meetings every week and she made sure to add the committee assignment to her company intranet profile, her LinkedIn profile, and her email signature.

Over the course of several months, Cassie was able to interact with the VP's on a number of occasions, and because she attended each week, her name was on each and every copy of the meeting minutes.

Five months later, when an Operations Director position was available, Cassie was invited to apply and interview for the position before the job opportunity was posted. By putting herself in a highly visible position and showing off her skills regularly, she was able to get the opportunity she wanted.

To get started on your visibility and consistency plan, you'll need to go back to your vision. Think about the goals you have for influence. Who needs to see you in order to reach that vision? Those people are your "audience."

You may also refer back to the Authority Planner to think about the 3 influential people in your industry and how they achieved visibility and consistency with their audience.

What did they do to get in front of the right people, and how often were they visible?

Visibility Planner

Who is your audience?

_____

_____

Where does your audience spend the most time?

_____

_____

What do you think is their favorite way to receive messages?

_____

_____

How can you reach your audience where they spend the most time in the way they want to receive you?

_____

_____

_____

What tools do you need to reach your audience with your messages?

_____

_____

_____

Consistency Planner

How regularly can you commit to connecting with your audience?

(Be realistic with your plan. Inconsistency can have the opposite effect and can create distrust.)

_____

_____

_____

How will you hold yourself accountable for achieving regularity?

(calendar reminders, a coach, a friend)

_____

_____

_____

What will you do if you can't meet your commitment?

_____

_____

_____

How will you communicate with your audience if you can't make a commitment?

_____

_____

_____

_____

Goal Setting

The next step in the process is planning your commitment to achieving your mission. Here are a few questions to help you plan your goals for reaching success.

How soon will you begin your plan for success?

_____

_____

_____

Who will partner with you on your journey?

_____

_____

_____

What's your timeline for achieving your goals?

_____

_____

_____

How will you stay committed?

_____

_____

_____

Your Journey Starts Here

Presence. Authority. Visibility. Consistency.

The principles you just learned illustrate the path that every great leader has had to take. No one becomes an influencer without first mastering all 4 of these principles. Influential people get noticed when they walk in a room, they have a resume to back-up their promises, and they're consistently visible — always where their audience needs them to be.

I hope this workbook has helped to bring clarity to your journey and has given you the tools you need to become the influential person you deserve to be.

Influence takes practice and depending on your goal it can take years to realize the results of your efforts. Your journey to influence will teach you about yourself, help you learn about others, and make you even more in tune with the world around you.

Thank you for letting me be a part of your journey to influence.
Keep in touch!

Krystal Covington, MBA